Audrey Evans
Not YouR OrdinaRy DoctoR

Written by **HEIDI BRIGHT BUTLER**

Illustrations by **JOYEETA NEOGI**

For scientists and caregivers like Audrey, Deb, and Rachel.

For the children whose lives depend on them.

For Amy, Kim, and Alex,

and especially for Andrew.

© 2019 Heidi Bright Butler
BRIGHT PAGES PUBLISHING
BREINIGSVILLE, PA

ISBN 978-0-578-57157-7
Library of Congress Control Number 2019915619
Evans, Audrey E., 1925–
Ronald McDonald House Charities.
Women in medicine--Juvenile literature.
Women scientists--Juvenile literature.
People with disabilities--Juvenile literature.
Cancer in children--Research--Juvenile literature.
Neuroblastoma--Treatment--Juvenile literature.
Biographies.
Chapter books.

Book design by Jodi Giddings
Illustrations by Joyeeta Neogi

Display font set in Lemon Lime Octopie and Gill Sans; main text set in Adobe Caslon Pro
Illustrations created in mixture of traditional and digital media

For book signings and presentations, email butlers5@ptd.net.

Hello.

Do you ever get in trouble?
When Audrey Evans was your age, she did.
She was often in trouble at home.
She didn't always do well in school.
No one expected she would become a doctor.
In this book you will find out how she surprised everyone
and grew up to do important things.

P.S.

The story is true!

P.P.S.

If you don't know the meaning of a word
in **dark ink**, turn to page 60 for help.

Contents

Chapter 1
Not Again!

Audrey didn't mean to get in trouble. She was ten when a neighbor lent her a horse so she could ride to her friend Jane's house. She dismounted *just* for a minute and the horse took off, heading down a railroad track. She was afraid it was going to get hit by a train. "Stop!" Audrey yelled, but the horse kept galloping.

A grown-up heard her and caught the horse. It was not hurt, but Audrey knew her parents would be mad. They wished she would be more careful. They did not know that when Audrey grew up, she would become famous for helping thousands of people. Even if they had known, she still would have been in trouble for letting the horse get away.

Chapter 2
How It All Began

Audrey was born in England on March 6, 1925. Life was very different then than it is today. There were no televisions, video games, or trampolines. Chocolate chips hadn't even been invented yet!

Audrey was the baby in her family. She had a sister named Mary and a brother named Pat. They lived near a very old city called York. Tourists from around the world still travel to York to see the wall Romans built around the city more than 1,000 years ago to keep invaders out. Part of the wall is still standing. You can walk on other walls that are hundreds of years old. You can also visit a castle.

Audrey did not live in the castle, but she did live in a big house. Taking care of it was a lot of work. Maids called "dailies" helped. Monday was wash day, Tuesday was ironing day, Wednesday was the day the upstairs got cleaned, Thursday was the day the downstairs got cleaned, and Friday was the day when most of the cooking got done. A **nanny** helped take care of the children.

Chapter 3
Hooray for Weekends

Saturday was one of Audrey's favorite days of the week. It was the day her father took her and Roger to York. Roger was the family dog—a Great Dane who was as tall as Audrey! When Audrey and her father stopped for a snack, Roger waited outside the shop. Audrey's dad always ordered a cup of coffee. Sometimes he let Audrey drink one too with lots of milk. That made her feel grown up, but hot chocolate tasted even better with the special **biscuits** she and her dad liked. Yum!

On Sundays Audrey walked to church with her father and brother. It was a long walk, but Audrey didn't mind. She loved spending time with her father. He was the head of the Sunday School and the director of the children's choir. After Sunday School Audrey and her brother walked home together while their father stayed for church. When her brother went away to boarding school, Audrey was too young to walk home by herself so she stayed with her dad. Sometimes she fell asleep in his lap during the sermon, but she always woke up for the singing!

Every night at bedtime Audrey said prayers with her mother. Her favorite went like this:

Jesus, tender shepherd, hear me.
Bless thy little lamb tonight.
Through the darkness be Thou near me.
Keep me safe til morning's light.

All this day thy hand has led me,
And I thank Thee for Thy care;
Thou hast clothed me, warmed and fed me,
Listen to my evening prayer.

Let my sins be all forgiven,
Bless the friends I love so well;
Take me, when I die, to heaven,
Happy there with Thee to dwell.

When she was little, Audrey could only say the first four lines of the prayer by heart. When she got older and memorized the rest, she was very proud of herself. She still didn't know what some of the words meant. She asked her mother what sins were. Her mom explained that sins are naughty things you do, and that you have to say you are sorry for them.

Audrey was naughty sometimes. She did not like to get dressed up for church. One Sunday morning her mom told her to change her clothes. She said what Audrey was wearing was not fancy enough. Audrey protested. "Jesus doesn't care what I wear," she said. "He sees me in the bath!" Audrey may have been right, but she still had to change her clothes and say "sorry" for talking back to her mother!

Audrey also should have said "sorry" to the nanny who helped to take care of her. In the afternoons Audrey was allowed to listen to a show called "The Children's Hour" on the radio. When it was over, her mother gave Audrey two treats—one for herself and one to take upstairs to her nanny. By the time Audrey got upstairs, sometimes the second treat had disappeared. Guess who ate it? Not the nanny!

Chapter 4
Trouble at School

Audrey didn't just get into trouble at home. When she was four years old, she started school at The Mount. The head of the school was Miss Waller. If you talked before prayers when you were supposed to be silent or if you talked in line going into the dining room, you got sent to Miss Waller's office. You had to sit on a bench outside until Miss Waller was ready to see you. Everyone who passed by knew you were in trouble. Audrey couldn't seem to stop talking even when she knew she should. She had to sit on that bench more than once!

Music was one of Audrey's favorite classes. You didn't have to be quiet there. Once after a concert Audrey's mother told her, "You certainly know how to play the drums. I could hardly hear anyone else." Audrey didn't realize that playing loudly was *not* the same as playing well.

When she was ten, Audrey went away to **boarding school** like her older sister and brother. She missed her parents, but she liked living with girls her own age. Traveling to school was an adventure. It took two to three hours by train to get there. For the first two years Audrey made the trip with her sister, but after her sister went to college, Audrey rode the train by herself. When she got to London—the biggest city in all of England—she had to change trains. **Porters** helped her find her way in the busy station.

Chapter 5

Adventures in the Country

Audrey loved summer vacations. Her family rented a cottage in the country. It did not have running water or electricity. Grown-ups took buckets to a well across the lane to get water for drinking and cooking. They collected rain water in big barrels and heated it over a fire in the fireplace once a week so the kids could take baths in a big round tub in the kitchen.

The children needed baths! They spent their days outside, playing and exploring. Audrey rode ponies for miles across the **moors**. Some days she met her parents for picnics by a pond where they could swim when the weather was hot.

When they weren't playing, the children helped out on a nearby farm, working with the field hands who stacked bales of straw on a wagon to be taken to the barn to provide bedding for the animals. When Audrey was only twelve, the farmer let her drive the wagon by herself. She took the reins of the two horses that pulled the cart and took off down a narrow dirt lane. The trip did not go as smoothly as she hoped. She hit a bump, and the wagon tipped. Luckily there were high **hedges** on both sides of the lane, so the cart did not flip all the way over. It just tilted on its side in the hedge. Audrey wasn't scared. She hopped out, climbed up on the other side of the wagon, and got it going again.

Another time when Audrey was driving a wagon, the horse came too close to a stone wall, and Audrey scraped her legs from top to bottom. The farmer's wife tried to wash the dirt out, but the cut got infected. Her mother had a fit. "Don't worry. It doesn't bother me," Audrey told her. "Well, it bothers me," her mother said. Sometimes Audrey's mother thought she was too wild, but she was a brave girl. She became a brave woman.

"I could easily have been killed from what I was allowed to do in the country," Audrey admitted when she was a grown-up. "It was outrageous, but it was a gorgeous life."

Chapter 6
Poor Audrey

When she was twelve, Audrey did almost die from what she did in the country. She got very sick from drinking raw milk. The milk you buy in stores is pasteurized. That means it has been heated up to get rid of germs. When Audrey was young, people who lived near farms often drank milk before it was pasteurized. If you did that, you could get a disease called tuberculosis. That is what happened to Audrey. She became so weak she had to stay in the hospital for almost a year.

Luckily, her mother had a part-time job helping out in the **pharmacy** at the hospital. She often came to Audrey's room to have lunch with her. There were no iPads then and very few televisions, but her father brought her books from the library every week. "Lying in bed was a bit boring, but I loved to read," Audrey said. "I had a radio and books and food, and I wasn't in pain. I just had to rest." Audrey tried to make the best of things, but she missed her sister and brother. She missed her friends. She even missed school. And she certainly missed playing outside.

Audrey never forgot what it felt like to be in the hospital as a little girl. When she grew up, she used that experience to help other children.

Chapter 7
"They're Only Clothes"

By the time Audrey got well, World War II had started. The government needed money to pay soldiers and to buy guns and tanks, so people weren't allowed to spend much on food and clothing. You could only buy things if you had coupons in your ration book.

Audrey needed clothes! She'd lost a lot of weight when she was sick, so all of her dresses were too big. Generous friends gave Audrey's parents their coupons so Audrey could get new clothes. She had fun shopping with her mother. They came home with pretty dresses that fit just right.

When Audrey was allowed to go back to school, her parents took her **trunk** filled with all her new clothes to the railroad station so it could be loaded onto the train the next morning, but during the night, enemy planes dropped a bomb on the station. Audrey's trunk was destroyed.

Audrey couldn't believe her beautiful clothes were gone. Her mother scolded her. "They're only clothes," she said. She told Audrey not to feel sorry for herself. The important thing was that no one was hurt. Audrey knew that, but she couldn't help feeling sad.

Chapter 8
Liar, Liar!

Even without new dresses, Audrey was excited to be back at school. Students had to keep a list of the books they read. By the end of the year Audrey had the longest list in the class—40 books! She was proud when she turned it in, but the **headmistress** did not think it was possible for her to have finished that many books. She called Audrey's parents and told them she was lying. Audrey's father came to school. He asked Audrey if she was telling the truth. She said "Yes!" and he believed her. He knew how much his daughter loved to read. Because the headmistress did not trust Audrey, her parents decided it would be best if she came home, so back to the Quaker school she went.

Chapter 9

Making the Best of a Bad Situation

England was still at war, and air raids were common. When a siren sounded, you had to run to the basement and hide in case your house got hit by a bomb. That was scary—*very* scary! Because enemy planes often flew over York, the students from the Quaker school were sent to live in a big house by the sea where they would be safe. Most of them were too young to realize how serious the war was. They thought it was fun to live at the beach!

On Saturdays the girls were allowed to go shopping in a nearby town. Audrey used her allowance to buy magazines. She built up a collection, and let other girls read them if they paid her **sixpence**. That gave her money to buy more magazines! Once when the school gardener was sick, she bought him a magazine. It was called *Country Life*. It was the perfect choice for a gardener. When she delivered it to his cottage, he was surprised and touched. Audrey had a caring heart.

Chapter 10
The War Hits Home

One day, right before the war ended, Audrey's family received terrible news. Her brother Pat had been killed. He was in the Royal Army Tank Corps, and his tank was hit by gunfire on the border between Holland and Germany. All eight soldiers inside the tank died. A soldier who worked with Pat came to visit Audrey's family. He told them that Pat had been very brave. Audrey and her parents were proud to hear that, but they still thought their hearts would break. They couldn't imagine life without Pat.

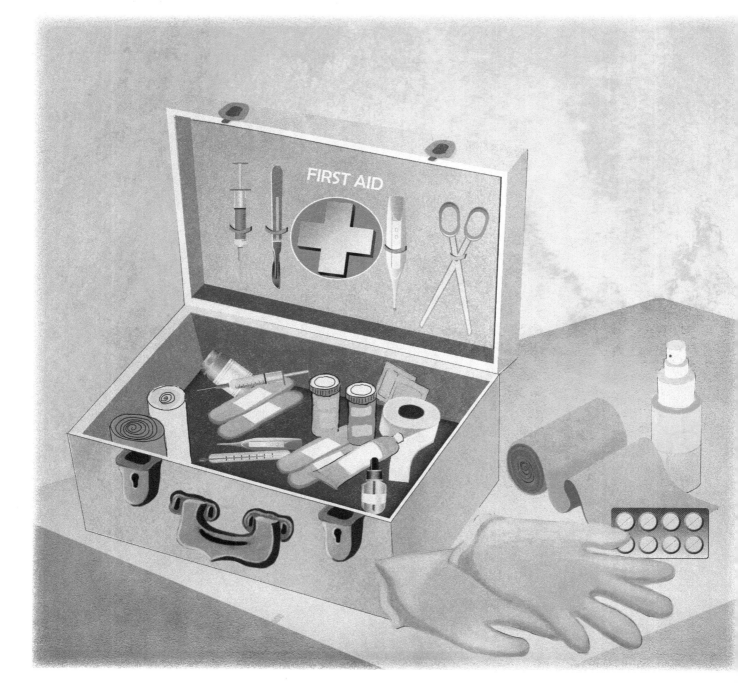

Chapter 11
Refusing to Give Up

Audrey wished she could have saved Pat. From the time she was very little, she wanted to be a doctor. When she was five, she made a first aid kit and carried it everywhere. It contained bandages, cotton balls, and an **antiseptic**. She didn't get to use it often, but if anyone got hurt, Audrey was eager to help.

Audrey's sister Mary also wanted to be a doctor. That was an unusual goal for girls at that time. Out of every 100 doctors, fewer than five were women. Some medical schools did not even accept women, but Mary was a good student. She got excellent grades. The whole family celebrated when she got a letter inviting her to study medicine at the University of Edinburgh in Scotland.

Audrey's mom and dad were thrilled for Mary, but they did not want Audrey to follow in her footsteps. She got sick too often. They didn't think she was strong enough to be a doctor. They encouraged her to be a nanny and to take care of children who were healthy. That was not what Audrey had in mind.

A friend of the family finally convinced Audrey's parents to give her a chance, but there was another problem. Audrey had missed a lot of school when she was in the hospital. She never really caught up. She flunked the test you needed to take to graduate from high school. How was she going to get into medical school now?

Audrey refused to give up. She spent an extra year at a special school called a **crammer** to get ready to take the test again. When exam day came, she must have been nervous, but this time she passed. Her hard work paid off.

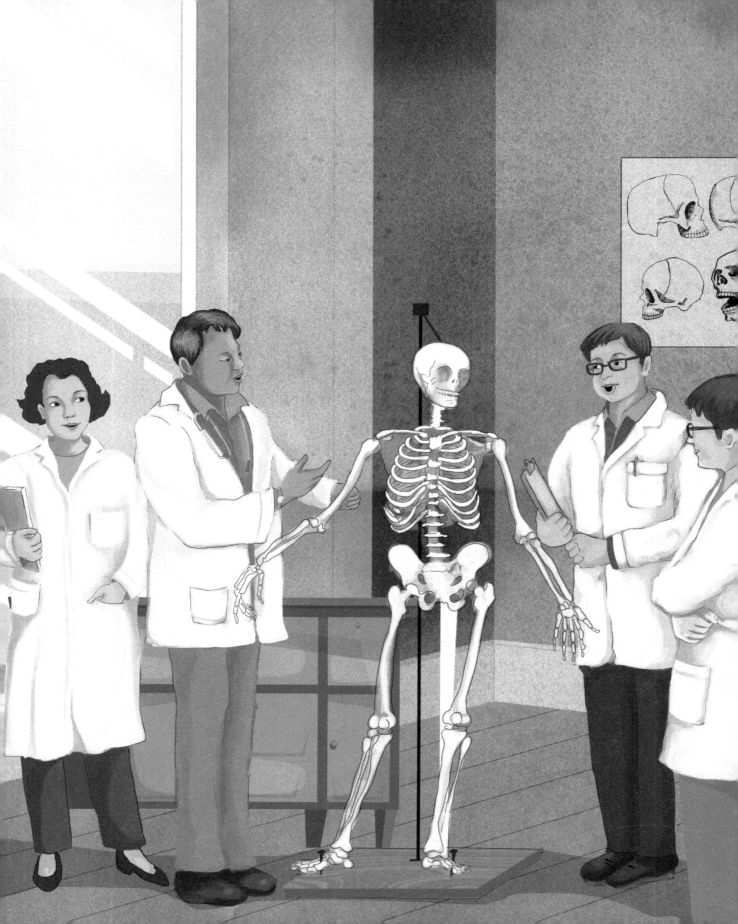

Chapter 12
Not Another F!

More good news followed. Audrey was accepted at the Royal College of Physicians and Surgeons in the same city in Scotland where her sister had studied medicine. Doctors there had heard how smart Mary was. They thought Audrey would do well, too, but Audrey did not do well. She flunked anatomy. Anatomy is the study of the human body. Understanding it is very important to becoming a doctor. Maybe Audrey needed to choose a different career.

No! Audrey was *determined* to become a doctor! When her teachers let her take the class again, she studied even harder. She still didn't do that well, but she *did* pass.

Audrey didn't understand why she was having so much trouble in school. What was wrong with her? A teacher solved the mystery. He discovered that Audrey had a learning disability. Because of the way her brain worked, it was hard for her to remember what she read, but she was good at remembering what she heard. If she had to answer questions about what was in a book, she did not do well, but she could remember what teachers said in class.

Audrey had to work harder than other students to pass her courses, but being a good listener made her good at helping patients. She could remember what patients told her about how they felt. And she was very good at figuring out how to help them get better. That was what mattered most. Even though her grades were not the best, her teachers had a feeling she would become a fine doctor. They were right.

Chapter 13
A Jolly Good Fellow

After doctors finish medical school, they must spend several years in a hospital, working with doctors who have more experience than they do. They used to have to live at the hospital in case they were needed in the middle of the night, so they were called "residents."

Audrey heard about a program that would allow her to begin her "residency" in another country. That sounded interesting. Very few doctors are chosen to participate, but Audrey took her chances and applied. Imagine how excited she was when she got a letter saying she had been picked! Soon she was heading to the United States as a Fulbright Fellow.

The journey took almost a week by boat. Day after day the passengers could not see a speck of land—only sea and sky—as they crossed the Atlantic, the second largest ocean in the world. When the ship finally docked, Audrey couldn't wait to explore. She was twenty-eight years old, and she had never been to America before.

Chapter 14
Life in America

Audrey did not know anyone in the United States, but she wasn't worried. She was confident she would make new friends. One of the first was Nancy Potter, a nurse who helped Audrey feel at home when she arrived at Boston Children's Hospital. Nancy and Audrey remained friends for the rest of their lives.

Doctors welcomed Audrey, too. She felt especially lucky to work with Sydney Farber, a doctor who was making important discoveries about cancer. Audrey got to see how he tested different medicines to find out which got the best results. She admired how much he cared for his young patients. He did everything he could to help them enjoy life even if they were sick. He even paid attention to their parents and their sisters and brothers. He knew that the whole family hurts when someone is ill.

Audrey worked long hours, but she did get a few days off. One weekend when another doctor and his wife were going out of town, they asked Audrey to take care of their children. She said she'd be glad to. Everything went well until Sunday morning. It was not just any Sunday. It was Easter. The children asked Audrey where the Easter bunny was. Audrey was puzzled. What was an Easter bunny? Audrey had no idea. When she was growing up in England, you sometimes colored hard-boiled eggs for Easter, but there was no Easter bunny. Audrey quickly called an American friend. The friend said, "Don't worry. Keep the children inside until after breakfast. Then send them out to the yard." When the children went outside, they found Easter eggs hidden all over. Audrey was amazed.

It was fun learning about American customs, but Audrey came to the United States to find out all she could about taking care of sick children so she could become a pediatrician. After two years in Boston, she moved to Baltimore, Maryland, to work with children at another famous hospital called Johns Hopkins before returning to Scotland to complete her residency.

Chapter 15
What a Shock!

In Baltimore Audrey met doctors like Helen Taussig who was the head of the pediatrics department, but when she went back to the hospital in Scotland, women residents weren't even allowed to eat dinner with the male residents to talk about what they were learning. Women had to eat in a separate dining room. One year there were no other women residents, so Audrey had to eat by herself every night. The waiter felt sorry for her and saved the best food for her. She never forgot how kind he was, but she knew women shouldn't be treated differently from men.

Other rules also were unfair. The hospital was huge. The male residents slept in rooms near the patients, but Audrey was assigned a room on the far side of the building. Every time there was an emergency it took her fifteen minutes to reach the person who was sick even if she walked or ran as fast as she could. That wasn't safe for patients. Audrey's boss agreed and found her a room nearby, but she had to share a bathroom with the men. She did not mind sharing, but the door did not have a lock. When Audrey took a bath, she had to sing loudly so no one walked in!

When Audrey's residency was over, she had to make a decision. In Scotland and England, only male pediatricians were hired to work in hospitals after their residencies. Women pediatricians were expected to get jobs in doctors' offices. If Audrey wanted to help the children who needed her the most—the ones who were the sickest—she would have to leave England.

Audrey wrote to the doctors she knew in Boston and asked if she could come back. They said yes, but they told her that the only job that was available was one other doctors didn't want because it was too sad. She would have to take care of children with cancer. In those days most kids with cancer died. Audrey took the job anyway. She knew Dr. Farber and others were making discoveries that would help those children.

Chapter 16
Chocolate Cake and Bongo Drums

Audrey lived near the hospital and ate all her meals there. She remembered what it was like to be stuck in a hospital room when she was a child, so she did not just stop in to see sick children once a day. She spent as much time as she could with them. They knew she cared about them. One time a little boy asked a nurse where Dr. Evans was. The nurse said, "I think she went to lunch." The boy said, "No, she didn't. She would have told me!"

Children trusted Audrey. Many of them felt they could talk with her about things their parents didn't want to talk about—things like dying. One boy asked her if he would be able to take his bongo drums to Heaven. Audrey said, "Sure you can. You can make a terrific noise in Heaven."

Audrey wished she could help every child get better, but when that wasn't possible, she did everything she could to make dying children happy. If a little boy was hungry for chocolate cake in the middle of the night, she would call down to the kitchen and ask that some be delivered to his room—even if it was midnight. The cooks couldn't believe it! One time she let a little girl keep a canary in her room. Other doctors may not have approved, but that didn't stop Audrey. She told the nurses and social workers, "Anything goes, as long as it isn't dangerous."

Some doctors thought they had the most important jobs in the hospital. Audrey disagreed. She believed that doctors, nurses, social workers, and **chaplains** needed to work together as a team to help children who were sick.

Chapter 17
Around the World with Audrey

Although she spent long hours at the hospital, Audrey knew you couldn't do good work if you were too tired. Everyone needed to take some time off. When she had a free weekend, she liked spending it with her friend Nancy and her family at their cabin on Lake Winnipesaukee, the biggest lake in New Hampshire. In the winter, they often went skiing.

Audrey also still loved horseback riding. One time she and a horse named Jim won a ribbon in a horse show. If you won a ribbon, you were supposed to ride around the ring one more time while people applauded. Jim was a young horse. Sometimes he was naughty like Audrey had been when she was young. When he was taking his victory lap around the ring, he started galloping so fast that Audrey was afraid he might not stop. Luckily a horse trainer saw what was happening. When Audrey and Jim reached the end of the lap, the trainer yelled, "Ho, Jim," and Jim walked calmly out of the ring. Audrey breathed a sigh of relief.

Another thing Audrey did for fun was to take trips. She often invited her friends' children to go with her. One year she took them to a ranch in Wyoming where they rode horses. Another year they went camping on Cape Cod. On that trip the children accidentally locked the keys in the car. They were worried that Audrey would be mad, but she was able to get the door open by sliding her credit card through the lock. She didn't even yell at them. She remembered what it was like to be a child who sometimes got in trouble!

When Audrey visited her friends in Scotland, she took the children to a farm like the one where she had spent summers. They stayed in a **boppy** with no electricity or running water, and they played in a **beck**, experiences they never forgot.

Audrey and the children traveled to other countries, too. They went to Greece, China and England to watch the best athletes in the world compete in horseback riding, **rugger** and other sports at the Olympics. One time they stayed at a house with a swimming pool with too much chlorine in it. By the end of the trip, the children's hair turned almost green! Their parents hardly recognized them when they got home. Trips were always an adventure with Audrey!

One of Audrey's favorite vacations was in Australia where she went scuba diving and explored the world's largest coral reef system. It's called the Great Barrier Reef. There you can see giant clams, jellyfish, octopuses and many different fish. Sharks live there, too. Audrey stayed away from sharks when she was diving, but one day when she was swimming, she spotted a large fin between herself and the beach. She was afraid to head for shore, so she kept swimming. So did the shark. Instead of panicking, Audrey used her head. She turned and started moving in the other direction. Luckily the shark did not. Audrey made it back to land safely. Whew!

Chapter 18
Detective Work

Audrey enjoyed vacations, but she had important work to do. Girls and boys were dying of cancer. She remembered how Dr. Farber had tried to find out which kinds of medicine worked best for kids with a kind of cancer called leukemia. Audrey wanted to do the same thing for children with a kind of cancer called neuroblastoma.

Audrey and other doctors decided to work together to solve the mystery. They gave some children with neuroblastoma one kind of drug. They gave other children a different drug. Some children got no medicine at all, and others got more than one kind of medicine.

Audrey kept careful records to see which children got better and which didn't. She made a surprising discovery. Many babies with neuroblastoma do not need to take medicine. They get well by themselves. Older children do need medicine. How much and what kind depend on how much cancer is in their bodies and where it is. Audrey put this information in a chart that doctors all over the world use to figure out how to help children with neuroblastoma get better. The chart is called the Evans Staging System. Doctors use it every day.

Chapter 19
The Fish on the Fourth Floor

A famous doctor named C. Everett Koop heard about the good work Audrey was doing. He was the head of The Children's Hospital of Philadelphia—one of the best children's hospitals in the country. He wanted Audrey to come there to help children with cancer. She said she would. She packed her bags and moved to Philadelphia.

One of the first things the people in charge of the hospital asked Audrey to do was to look at plans for an addition that would give them space to take care of more children. Audrey did not like what she saw. The rooms were boring.

How about a floor-to-ceiling birdcage—with a tree in it? And a wall-to-wall fish tank full of colorful fish? Watching birds and fish would help take children's minds off their troubles.

Was she crazy? A hospital was not a zoo! "And what about the cost," her new bosses said. "Don't worry," Audrey replied, "I will find the money." She called someone she knew who cared a lot about sick children. That person said she would be glad to pay for the giant birdcage and the fish tank.

When other hospitals heard about what Audrey had done, they started looking for ways to make being in their hospitals more fun. Audrey led the way.

Chapter 20
Teaming up with the Eagles

Families traveled to The Children's Hospital of Philadelphia from all over the country so their children could get special care. Parents wanted to stay nearby so they could visit their children, but hotel rooms were expensive. If a mom or a dad didn't have enough money, sometimes Audrey paid the bill herself. She knew it was important for parents and children to be together when a child was sick.

One day a man named Jimmy Murray asked if he could meet with Audrey. Audrey had never heard of Jimmy. Her secretary told her that Jimmy worked for the Philadelphia Eagles. Audrey had never heard of them either. Her secretary explained that the Eagles were a football team.

Audrey couldn't imagine why someone from a football team wanted to meet with her. She found out that one of the players' daughters had cancer. Her name was Kim Hill. When Kim got better, the players and the team's owner—Leonard Tose—were so happy that they wanted to do something to help other children get well. They raised money for the hospital and brought Audrey a check for $125,000.

$125,000 is a lot of money! Audrey was polite. She said thank you, but when the Eagles were getting ready to leave, she told them she needed more money! They did not expect that, but when she explained her idea, they knew it was a good one. She wanted enough money to buy a house near the hospital where families could stay to be close to their children.

Jimmy Murray thought hard. He came up with a plan. He knew that children loved to eat at McDonald's. One of the Eagles' best players—Bill Bergey—was featured in commercials for the "Shamrock Shakes" McDonald's sold around St. Patrick's Day. Shamrock Shakes were green, just like the Eagles' uniforms. Jimmy got in touch with Ed Rensi, a manager at McDonald's. He asked Ed if the money made from Shamrock Shakes could be used to buy a house for families of kids with cancer. Ed said yes.

The plan worked! Audrey found a house for sale near the hospital. A builder named John Caruso whose daughter had cancer helped fix the house up so that families would be comfortable there. The first Ronald McDonald House opened in Philadelphia on October 15, 1974. Today there are more than 300 Ronald McDonald houses around the world. Millions of families have stayed there while their children got well.

Chapter 21
Wedding Bells

Audrey loved children. She would like to have had some of her own, but that didn't work out. She had boyfriends when she was young. She thought she was going to marry one of them, but he married someone else. Audrey was sad at the time, but she still had a good life. She enjoyed her work, and she got to be with children every day. Some of them came to visit her even after they grew up.

And guess what? Audrey *did* get married! When she was 79 years old, she married another doctor who was famous for helping children with cancer. His name was Giulio D'Angio. His nickname was Dan. They had worked together and been friends for many years. They got married at an Episcopal church early one weekday morning. They went out to breakfast to celebrate with a few friends, and then they went to their laboratories and got back to work. They still wanted to learn more about cancer.

Audrey and Dan lived in an apartment high above Philadelphia where they had a beautiful view of the city. Can you believe they had a garden on the 18th floor? They did! It was out on their balcony.

They loved animals, but they didn't like it when birds made nests in their garden. They shooed them away. They were worried that baby birds would get killed if they fell to the sidewalk from the 18th floor while they were learning to fly. They cared as much about animals as they did about people.

Audrey and Dan didn't have pets, but they kept dog biscuits by their front door. When Dan went for walks, he put the biscuits in his pocket. He gave them to the dogs in the neighborhood as treats. The dogs loved to see him coming!

Chapter 22
More to Do

Audrey and Dan did not retire until they were in their eighties. Audrey had worked as a doctor for more than 50 years. When she retired, she missed helping children. She did not just want to sit around. She and her minister, Fr. Sean Mullen, started a middle school for children who live in a poor section of Philadelphia, so they could get a good education.

Just as Audrey wasn't an ordinary doctor, the Episcopal day school she co-founded wasn't an ordinary school. The St. James School is open 10–11 hours every day and sometimes on Saturdays, even in the summers. Students have to study hard, but they also have a chance to take music and dance lessons, to learn how to cook healthy meals, run races, ride horses, row boats, build robots, to believe in themselves, and to help other people.

When Audrey turned 90, the children at the school had a birthday party for her. There was a big cake and lots of balloons. Audrey loved every minute of it. She could hardly wait to turn 91!

Chapter 23
You Can Help Too

Audrey Evans is famous for many things—for helping children with cancer, for starting the Ronald McDonald houses, and for creating St. James School. She won a lot of awards, but what she hopes people will remember about her is not the awards. It is that she was a woman who cared.

Because she cared, the world is a better place.

You can make the world a better place, too. Maybe you will build houses. Maybe you will be a teacher. Maybe you will grow food for people who are hungry. Maybe you will come up with a new invention. If you aren't successful at first, don't give up. Keep trying. That's what Audrey did. And be sure to have fun, too. That's what Audrey would say!

Audrey's Scrapbook

Audrey was the youngest in her family. Here she is with (left-right) her brother Pat, her sister Mary, the nanny, and her parents.

What a cutie! Audrey was about three years old in this picture.

Down, boy! When the family dog stood on his hind legs, he was almost as tall as Audrey's dad!

Look who won a ribbon!

Except where noted otherwise, all of these pictures are from Audrey's personal collection.

(Left) In this picture, Audrey is getting ready to go scuba diving with some friends. What will they see under the sea?

Is this Little Bo Peep? No! It's Audrey helping to tend the sheep on her godson's farm in Scotland.

Not many women did cancer research when Audrey first started. This picture was taken in 2000 at a meeting of doctors trying to find a cure for neuroblastoma. (Photo courtesy of Advances in Neuroblastoma Research Association. Photo taken by C. P. Reynolds, M.D., Ph.D.)

What a happy day it was when Audrey and Dan got married! When they went out to breakfast to celebrate, Audrey's long-time friend Nancy Potter surprised them with streamers. (Photo by Barbara Alton)

All smiles! Audrey with students from the school she helped to found in Philadelphia. (Photo courtesy of the St. James School)

Glossary

Children in the United States and children in England all speak English, but sometimes they have trouble understanding each other. If you ask, "Where is the boot," a boy from England might point to the trunk of a car, while a girl from the United States might show you what she's wearing on her feet.

Here are some words you might not have heard before:

Antiseptic: An antiseptic is medicine you put on a cut so it won't get infected. Sometimes it stings. Ouch!

Beck: You can wade in a beck. It is a creek.

Biscuits: In the United States, biscuits are breads eaten with meals. In England, they are cookies or crackers.

Boarding school: Would you like to live at school? Children who go to boarding school stay there overnight. Sometimes they have their own room. Sometimes they share a room with another student their age. The students eat, play, and study together. There are some boarding schools in the United States. One boarding school in England started more than 1,000 years ago!

Boppy: In the United States a boppy is a pillow for babies. In England it is a cottage.

Chaplain: A chaplain is a minister who works at a hospital or in a school.

Crammer: Audrey went to a "crammer" after high school to get ready to study at a university. That school helped her "cram" a lot of knowledge into her head in a short period of time.

Headmistress: At some schools, a principal is called a headmistress or a headmaster.

Hedges: You've seen a hedge! They are made up of bushes that grow together to form a border to a yard. There are lots of them in England.

Moors: Moors are hilly areas that are not fit for farming. They can go for miles. The land is often wet. There are lots of moors in Scotland and some in England. There are not many in the United States.

Nanny: Some families hire a nanny to help take care of the children. Have you heard of Mary Poppins?

Pharmacy: A store where medicines are kept.

Porters: A person whose job is to help carry luggage.

Rugger: A nickname for rugby, a very popular sport in England. It is kind of like football, but sometimes the players throw the ball backwards!

Sixpence: The English say "pence" instead of "pennies." Sixpence are no longer used in England, but if you go to England (or Ireland, Scotland, or Wales) you can still get coins worth one pence, two pence, five pence, ten pence, twenty pence, and fifty pence. Which would you rather have?

Trunk: A trunk is like a large suitcase.

It might be fun to surprise your family and friends by using some of these words.

Selected Bibliography

Most of the information in this book came from Audrey. What fun it was to interview her in her apartment with its breathtaking view of the city of Philadelphia! Her husband Dan would bring us coffee and biscuits to snack on as we chatted. It was obvious how much they loved each other.

Before interviewing Audrey, I read everything I could about her. Below you will find a list of some articles you might enjoy. If you would like to "meet" Audrey, ask your parents if you can watch these videos on YouTube:

www.youtube.com/watch?v=hstjG19OjkA
With Julia Fisher Farbman of the Modern Hero series

www.youtube.com/watch?v=hVZRsY07oIQ
With Susan Campbell of the Ronald McDonald House of Philadelphia

Books

Steve McWilliams and Jimmy Murray. *Life is an Audible: The Jimmy Murray Story*. Harrowood Books, 2019.

Electronic Sources

Advances in Neuroblastoma Research Association. "ANR Meetings Photo Galleries—Philadelphia 2000." www.anrmeeting.org/galleries/gallery-2000.php. Slide 20. Texas Tech University Health Sciences Center (2008-2018). (accessed August 29, 2019).

U.S. National Library of Medicine. "Changing the Face of Medicine. Dr. Audrey Elizabeth Evans." cfmedicine. nlm.nih.gov/physicians/biography_106.html. First published 2003. Updated 2018.

"St. James School. "Dr. Audrey Evans Co-Founder and Visionary." https://stjamesphila.org/dr-audrey-evans. (accessed October 25, 2019.)

WHYY. "Dr. Audrey Evans Continues to Inspire Others Beyond Retirement." whyy.org/articles/audrey-evans/. March 26, 2013.

Acknowledgments

Audrey knew that everyone who works at a hospital or at a school has an important job to do. The same is true of writing a book. Here are some of the people who helped to create this book.

Audrey—Thank you for sharing your story. Thanks, too, to Giulio D'Angio, John Maris, Barbara Alton, and Kate Schneider for facilitating the conversations and the research.

Joyeeta Neogi—Thank you for the beautiful (and funny) drawings. You live in India. I live in the United States. Computers enabled us to work together even though we have never met. The same is true of Jodi Giddings who married the illustrations and the words in the book without the benefit of coffee.

Allison Wortche—Thank you for insights about the world of publishing and for editing the manuscript with the skill of a surgeon. Donna Shoemaker—There aren't enough PEEPS® in Bethlehem to thank you for being the nicest and pickiest nitpicker ever.

CorinaLynn Scholl—Thank you for lugging your scanner through the streets of Philadelphia on a hot summer day to get photographs for the book.

Paul Acampora, Carol Henn, Katherine Noll, Emily Bright Krusack, Janet Lawler, Barbara Love, Vicki Mayk, and Cora Aquino Yockers—Thank you for being writers who assist and encourage other writers.

Thank you to the children who helped select the artist and read rough drafts of the story. Your suggestions made the book better. High fives to Gavin Clough; Regan Dittmar; James Henry; Elise, Felix, Jolie, and Lily Eyvazzadeh; Leila Gamboa; Savanah Halimolij; Khadeeja Hussain; Aiden, Evelyn and Maddie Lindsay; Liam McCarthy; Bryce and Colby Salapek; Aiden Schankel; Shreya Singh; and Arwen del Real Sobiech.

There should be a steep fine for not expressing gratitude to librarians. Thank you to Anne Bittner, Cris Bright, Olga Conneen, and Pamela Saunders for providing practical tips about the best ways to make Audrey's story accessible. A similar shout out to Melissa Koberlein and the students in her self-publishing class at Northampton Community College, to Bob Graeff who knows a thing or two about education, and to medical guru Camille Eyvazzadeh.

Susan Huber Horesta and Katherine Kidd—Thank you for your suggestions and words of encouragement. Always.

Thank you to Harriet and Richard Bright for being parents who read to your children, made sure we got a good education, and insisted that even when something is hard, it is worth doing.

Larry Butler—Thank you for putting up with my compulsion to drop everything when The Muse speaks.

Megan and Britt—As Audrey pointed out, siblings often get overlooked when their brother or sister gets sick. Thank you for all you did for your brother and for us when you were hurting too.

Andrew—Thank you for your love, your jokes, and your courage. We miss you still.

CPSIA information can be obtained
at www.ICGtesting.com
Printed in the USA
LVHW071101100320
649569LV00016B/58

9 780578 571577